LET THERE BE
FACEBOOK

Status Updates from God, Gaga, and Everyone in Between

AN UNAUTHORIZED PARODY

Travis Harmon

& Jonathan Shockley

A TOUCHSTONE BOOK

Published by Simon & Schuster

New York   London   Toronto   Sydney   New Delhi

Touchstone
A Division of Simon & Schuster, Inc.
1230 Avenue of the Americas
New York, NY 10020

First Touchstone trade paperback edition November 2011

TOUCHSTONE and colophon are registered trademarks of Simon & Schuster, Inc.

For information about special discounts for bulk purchases,
please contact Simon & Schuster Special Sales at 1-866-506-1949
or business@simonandschuster.com.

The Simon & Schuster Speakers Bureau can bring authors to your live event.
For more information or to book an event contact
the Simon & Schuster Speakers Bureau at 1-866-248-3049
or visit our website at www.simonspeakers.com.

Designed by Ruth Lee-Mui

Photo credits appear on pages 147–48.

Manufactured in the United States of America

1   3   5   7   9   10   8   6   4   2

ISBN 978-1-4516-5943-6
ISBN 978-1-4516-5945-0 (ebook)

For Mark Zuckerberg.

We should hang!

Introduction

What you now hold in your hands (yes, this book) is more important than anything you've ever held in your hands before. (Yes, even that. That too!) In fact, we state unequivocally that this book is the most important thing ever. Because it changes history. Because it *is* history. History is now this book. History is now Facebook. And what could be more important than Facebook? Nothing. Not a goddamned thing. Let there be Facebook! Let there be *Let There Be Facebook*.[1]

Confused? Of course you are. Allow us to break it down: We recently discovered that past generations connected with each other via a crude internet-like system called the Ethernets. And as we explored the ancient Ethernets,[2] we found something even more staggering: Facebook. Historical

---

[1] There are but a few reasonable reactions to a discovery of this magnitude, and fainting is one of them. Please, have a seat. Lie down if you must. There is no shame in the light-headedness one feels when confronted with our enormous find.

[2] How did the Ethernets work? An abacus was involved. Also, a series of pulleys and nozzles; electrician's tape; and, yes, the efforts of a time-traveling Mark Zuckerberg. Apparently, at some point in the near future, Zuckerberg will realize that he can create further riches if Facebook had existed since the dawn of time. Zuckerberg then commands his Palo Alto brain trust to set to work on an ad-supported time machine. Trusting no underling with so important a task, Zuckerberg himself travels back to the big bang. Once there, he mines the interests and personal information of evolving mitochondria and primordial muck, then monetizes his way up the evolutionary ladder, engorging his revenue stream until the world ends in 2012. (Of course, as always, the story isn't quite so simple. Zuckerberg is pursued throughout the timescape by the litigious Winklevoss twins, who operate a time machine bought for them by their daddy. Zuckerberg must constantly leap to and fro throughout the centuries in order to duck summonses. But we digress.)

figures using Facebook. Facebook is not just the perfect platform for sharing mankind's most precious thoughts, mindless prattle, and links to cat vids. It is also immortal.[3] Facebook has been wasting creation's time since time was created. Yes, we found history's Facebook. We fully expect to clean up at this year's Historian Awards.[4]

And so, thanks to *Let There Be Facebook* and the colossal, earthshaking discoveries contained within, the past is more accurate, accessible, and annoyingly acronymed than ever. Then, as now, Facebook demands a public display of naked self-absorption and obsession with the minutiae of one's life. And it's all here—the interests, friend requests, inane interactions, and constant spelling mistakes of history's most famous participants. Historical figures—they're just like us![5]

Here are just a few examples of the massive revelations we've carefully selected for *Let There Be Facebook:*

- Just as the modern-day Facebooker might lament the lack of Chunky Monkey at the grocery store, Joan of Arc took time to complain "FML" while being burned alive.

- Julius Caesar was much frattier than previously thought. We've uncovered his last known correspondence before his assassination: a booty call to Cleopatra. Caesar's last post not only reveals previously unknown ancient Latin syntax and slang but also grants us insight into his inner bro.

- Jonah and the Whale is no religious myth. Not only did Jonah exist, he apparently had enough knowledge of the Lonely Island's oeuvre to reference "I'm on a Boat."

So forget everything you thought you knew about history. Throw away those cave wall paintings. Toss out those ancient songs and elaborate

---

[3] Like *Highlander.*
[4] The Historian Awards, or Histies, honor the year's greatest historical findings and research. Ironically, no one knows when they were first held.
[5] Except historical figures' use of Facebook often led to much more bloodshed, enslavement, and torture.

dance traditions. Shred those yellowed documents rescued from monasteries. Burn the museums. Fire the professors. This book is all the history you need. The information contained in *Let There Be Facebook* is just as authentic, accurate, and important as the information we share on Facebook today![6]

You're welcome.
Dr. Tony Cougarmouth
Brylon K. Tilgh, Ph.D.
Smyrna, TN
June 26, 2011

Dr. Tony Cougarmouth and Brylon K. Tilgh, Ph.D., are professors of Social Networking and History People at Central Southern Middle Tennessee State University in Moak Table, TN.

[6] Which is to say really, really important.

LET THERE BE
FACEBOOK

God

God
Let there be light.

Big Bang OK sure thing.

God
This is good.

Big Bang I guess, if you think the universe expanding rapidly is good, yeah, sure.

God
Let there be a firmament in the midst of the waters, and let it separate the waters from the waters.

Big Bang Dude, the universe is just cooling, which leads to expansion.

God
And it is so.

Big Bang Duh.

God
Let the earth put forth vegetation, plants yielding seed, and fruit trees bearing fruit in which there is seed, each according to its kind, upon the earth.

Big Bang Whoa! Slow up, man. We got a few billion years to go! Let's not rush this shizz.

God

Let there be lights in the firmament of the heavens to separate the day from the night, and let them be signs for seasons and for days and years, and let the lights in the firmament of the heavens give light upon the earth.

Big Bang Lights in the firmament of the heavens? You mean the collapsing molecular clouds that will eventually become stars? Have you ever even read a book?

God Listen, Poindexter, nobody likes a know-it-all. I'm trying to make something here and you're ruining it for everybody.

Big Bang I'm just doing my thing.

God Do your thing, bro, but lose the attitude.

Big Bang You're the one taking credit for someone else's work over here.

God That's blasphemy, chief. You're cruising for a smiting.

Big Bang You can't smite a theory.

God Forget this. I'm gonna make some people.

Big Bang See, you're all "I'm gonna make this" when it's the scientific processes that started with me that will result in the birth of humankind.

God Whatever. I'm the one that gets to mess with 'em.

God is now friends with **Adam**.

Adam

 God
Sup, big guy?

 Adam Just chillin'. Enjoying some peace and quiet. Hey, thanks again for making me.

 God NP, dude. Li'l worried tho, bro. You got to get out of the house.

 Adam A house is what now?

 God
You know what you need?

 Adam Nothin'. I'm good.

 God A woman.

 Adam A woman is what now?

 God
Little action would fix you right up.

 Adam Srsly, brah, I'm tip-top. Just got made. Hanging out in the garden with all the nargs and littlenargs.

 God Those are trees and bushes.

Adam Are you not keeping the names I came up with? I spent a lot of time on those.

 God
Tonight when you're asleep I'm going to make you a little friend out of your rib.

 Adam Uh . . . that doesn't even make sense.

 God You can thank me later.

 Adam For a rib monster?

Adam became friends with **Eve** using the **Only Other Person on Earth Finder**.

 Adam is in a relationship with **Eve**.

 God
You guys are going to have a blast. Just as long as you don't, um . . . let me pick something arbitrarily here . . . don't eat this certain fruit.

 Adam A fruit is what now?

 God Formerly known as nargbuttons.

 Adam I SPENT A LOT OF TIME COMING UP WITH THOSE NAMES!

Eve invited **Adam** to a **Fruit-Eating Party**.

Fruit-Eating Party

Adam was invited by **Eve**

When	The Birth of Shame
Where	Tree of Knowledge
Creators	Eve, Serpent
Info	Bring your appetite! And something to cover up your filthy, filthy body.

Will Be
There

 Eve

 Serpent

 Adam

 Sexist Overtones

Might Be
There

 Wrath of God

 Animals Who Suddenly Want to Eat Each Other

 Eve posted a pic.

Best thing I've ever tasted. Sweet, juicy, plus I am so aware of my naked vagina right now.

 Serpent Toldja!

 Adam Are you having an affair with that snake?

 Eve GTFO. He's totally gay.

 Serpent Everybody says that. I think it's because I got nice legs.

Adam is attending **Fruit-Eating Party**.

Adam
Why didn't anybody tell me you could totally see my dick?

Eve You mean penis?

Adam I'm sticking to my guns on this one.

God is attending **Fruit-Eating Party**.

God
Nice fig leaves, a-holes. I can still see your junk.

Adam Dang.

Eve FML.

God
You can't even follow one capricious rule? If you aren't going to stay stupid, then you'll have to work yourselves to death and painfully crap out babies.

Adam FML.

Eve Dang.

Serpent Sucks to be you. LOL

God And gimme those legs!

Serpent But what am I going to do with all these shoes?

Abraham

God
Hey, you busy?

 Abraham Sup.

 God Kill your kid.

 Abraham WTF?

 God Do it.

 Abraham And I would want to kill my kid why?

 God 'Cause I said so.

 Abraham Can't argue with that logic.

 God LOL, srsly, kill him.

 Abraham JK I'll kill him.

God Kill him good.

 Abraham I wouldn't do this for anybody else!

 God Actions, not words.

 Abraham Should I bash his little head in with a rock?

 God Nah, jes' stab him, then burn him up.

 Abraham OK, but you owe me.

 God I see a lot of Facebook-postin' but no Isaac-killin'.

 Abraham
OK, my son's all tied up to the firewood. Gonna stab him and then set him on fire. Wish me luck!!

 Angel Hold up, dude, God's totally messing with you.

 Abraham You ass.

 God LOL

 Angel LOL, hilarious you were totally going to do it.

God Father of the year over here.

 Abraham ROFL You guys!

 Angel Father's Day'll be slim pickin's at your house.

 Abraham LOL You guys are evil.

 God Hey, watch it.

 Abraham Sorry.

Noah

Work and Education

Employer   God (40 days ago–present)

Beliefs and Values

Religion   Jewish

Politics   All politicians are now drowned, but I saved rats. Do the math.

Quotes   "You're crazy!"—a lot of dumb a-holes who are under water right now.

Favorites

Movies   Evan Almighty, Hard Rain, Dr. Dolittle (Eddie Murphy version)

Music   They Might Be Giants' Flood, Elvis Costello's Shipbuilding, Phish

Sports   Shuffleboard

Hobbies and Pastimes

Doing Crazy $!!@ God Tells Me To, Arks, Animals (for procreation purposes only—nothing kinky)

Basic Information

About Noah   Sorry I didn't have room on the ark for dinosaurs. They are really big.

Contact Information

Look for the boat.

News Feed

 God ▶ **Job** You're the best, brah! You love me so much!

 Job True dat.

 Satan ▶ **God** Your boy Job is only into you because you gave him so much cool swag.

 God You wish! He's my brah, bro!

 Satan Wanna mess with him?

 God Absolutely.

 Satan is Messing with **Job**.

 Job WTF? All my livestock and servants were killed or stolen or burned alive today! FML!

 Satan Also, a house fell on your kids and killed 'em. Man, when it rains it pours, huh?

 Job Everything I have has been taken from me!

 Satan I bet you feel like cursing God right now, huh?

Job Nope! God's awesome. He giveth and he taketh away.

 Satan *rolls eyes*

 Satan You heard the part about your dead kids, right?

 God ▶ Satan See? Got the dude whipped.

 Satan Let me give him boils or something.

 God What is it with you and boils?

 Satan I dunno, they just really work for me.

 God OK, but don't kill him.

 Satan Why not?

 God That would be cruel.

 Satan gave **Job** Sore Boils from the Sole of His Foot unto His Crown

 Job
Ow.

 Job's Wife Have you thought about just goin' screw it, cursing God, and dying?

Job Have you thought about shutting the hell up?

 Job
Just sitting on some ash and jabbing at my rotted skin with broken pottery.

God is attending **Job's Pity Party**.

 Job likes this.

 God
Job, u my dawg cos u never got all "whatever" on me even when you got butt boils. So I'm gonna give u back all yr shizz only better.

 Job You'll bring my kids back to life?

 God No. All right, I'm outtie. Goin' to hit up Outback Steakhouse 'cause Satan totally owes me a Bloomin' Onion.

 Job For what?

 God Um . . . nuthin'.

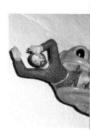

Jonah

 Jonah
I'm in a whale, bitch!

 God You trippin'! That's no whale. That's a great fish.

 Jonah Meh . . . he ain't so great.

The Pyramids

The Pyramids
Want to give a quick shout-out to everybody who built us. Thanks a lot!

 Pharaohs No problem.

 Slaves Our pleasure!

 Skilled Craftsmen You're welcome!

 Foreign Workers You betcha!

 Aliens Zeep Zorp!

Alexander the Great

 Alexander the Great
Let us head east to protect our northern borders!
We shall defeat the Thracians and the Triballians!

 Macedonian Army Sounds like a plan.
Shouldn't take too long.

 Alexander the Great
Good job! Who's up for securing Illyria and the
Taulanti?

 Macedonian Army Sure! Let's knock it
out.

 Alexander the Great
Decided we should head south and smack up on
Thebes.

 Macedonian Army Um . . . OK, why not?

 Alexander the Great
Since we're already headed south, let's just keep
going into Asia Minor!

 Macedonian Army Alexanderrrrrrrrrrrrrrrrr!
We're tiiii-red!

 Alexander the Great
We're in the neighborhood . . . Syria, here we come!

 Macedonian Army Can we go home yet?
We have to go to the bathroom!

Alexander the Great You just went to the bathroom during the siege of Tyre!

 Alexander the Great
You know who needs some good conquering? Egypt!

 Macedonian Army Conquering Egypt is STUPID.

 Alexander the Great
There is no way I'm this close and not gonna take Babylon.

 Macedonian Army We think you have a problem.

 Alexander the Great
Persia! Come on guys, Persia! We GOT to have Persia! I just GOTTA have it!

 Macedonian Army Has anyone ever told you that you might have an addiction?

 Alexander the Great
Just Central Asia. Central Asia, that's it. I swear to God I'm quitting after Central Asia.

 Macedonian Army Look, this isn't anything as formal as an intervention, but you can't keep doing this to yourself. To US, man. To those you care about.

 Alexander the Great
I know I sound like a broken record, but India is so nice this time of year, and I thought, just one more time, then I can really quit for good . . .

 Macedonian Army We left.

 Alexander the Great MORE FOR ME.

Cleopatra

 Cleopatra is Queen of Egypt.

 Cleopatra is married to her 12-year-old brother Ptolemy XIII

 Cleopatra It's a tradition!

 Ptolemy XIII Girls are gross. LOL

 Cleopatra
Another lonely night on FB now that my brother/husband (brosband?) and his eunuch advisor have banished me.

 Julius Caesar U lookin' fine as hell. Want to hook up?

 Cleopatra Txt me your digits.

 Cleopatra is in a relationship with **Julius Caesar**.

 Cleopatra It's weird to be with someone I'm not related to.

 Soothsayer Beware the Ides of March!

 Julius Caesar @Soothsayer F you.

Cleopatra Honey, don't feed the trolls.

Julius Caesar
Hey, babe, wut u up 2? I'm chillin' with my budz in the Senate. Just found out it's Bring Your Knife Day. Didn't get the memo, LOL

 Cleopatra Oh shit.

 Cleopatra and **Julius Caesar** are no longer in a relationship.

 Marc Antony U lookin' fine as hell.

 Cleopatra Txt me your digits.

 Cleopatra is in a relationship with **Marc Antony**.

 Marc Antony I don't mind sloppy seconds!

 Cleopatra LOL I often enter into relationships for strategic purposes.

 Marc Antony I did it all for the nookie.

 Cleopatra Gross! LOL

 Marc Antony
Hey, wanna watch me kick Octavian's butt?

 Cleopatra Go get 'im, sweetie!

 Octavian
I just kicked your boyfriend's butt and then he killed himself.

Marc Antony I'm a sore loser. LOL

 Cleopatra Great. Now I have to kill myself. Thanx a lot, a-hole.

Cleopatra posted a new photo to her album **Suicide Pics**.

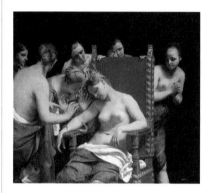

Having second thoughts. Anybody know what to do for a snakebite?

 Octavian Yow!

 Cicero BOING!

 Asp Anything more than a mouthful is a waste. LOL

 Cleopatra Grow up, you guys! A snake just bit my boobie.

Spartacus

Spartacus
I'm Spartacus.

Another Slave I'm Spartacus.

Another Slave I'm Spartacus.

Another Slave I'm Spartacus.

Romans WTF

The Last Supper

Jesus invited you

Time	A.D. 33-ish
Location	The Upper Room; if we can't get a table, there's a Chipotle across the street.
More Info	Bring your appetite! Also, one of you will betray me.

13 Attending
Jesus
His Disciples

Not Attending
Regular Jews

James
Man, had a great time last night, guys. We really need to do that more often!

Peter I can't deny a fun time was had by all! LOL

Andrew What a meal!

James It got a little weird toward the end but I wasn't gonna let that ruin my night.

Phillip I've had a moist towelette handed to me after dinner, but a foot wash? Wow! Thanks, Jesus!

John Great bread!

Matthew You mean body. LOL!

Simon The wine must have been that high dollar stuff!

 Thomas I doubt it.

 Thaddeus You mean blood, LOL!

 Bartholomew Gross!

 Judas I don't know what the hell you guys are talking about. I had a shitty evening.

Jesus Feed

 Matthew ▶ Bartholomew I'm really worried! I haven't seen Jesus all day!

 Bartholomew Do you think somebody ratted him out?

 Thomas Who would do something like that?

 Judas posted a new pic.

New Jet Ski, suckaz!

 Simon Damn, son! How much that cost u?

 Judas Got it for less than 30.

 Thaddeus What u do, rob a bank LOL??

Judas LMFAO not exactly.

 John Sell Jesus out to the authorities?

 Judas . . .

 Bartholomew That is so Judas.

 Judas Prophecy! The divine plan to save mankind! Just playin' my part! It was foretold by God!

 Thomas It was foretold for you to buy a Jet Ski?

 Judas It wasn't foretold for me not to buy a Jet Ski . . .

A Long, Pleasant Life of Safety and Security Ending in a Peaceful, Non-Sudden Death

Pompeii has invited you

20,000
Attending

 Lovers of Life

 Sex Mural Enthusiasts

Not Attending

 People Who Understand How Volcanoes Work

When:	Whenever. We're gonna be here for a long, long time.
Where:	Right underneath the seething volcano.
Info:	Come settle down with us! Enjoy beautiful Mediterranean Sea vistas, erotic art, and stunning views of Mount Vesuvius. New starter homes perfect for young families.

Pompeii Lady
Looking to put down some roots. Pompeii sounds perfect! Great place for kids to grow up.

Pompeii Dude
Took early retirement. Looking forward to spending my golden years in tranquility. Life is just beginning!

Pompeii Lady
Just opened up a new savings account for my kids. Never too soon to start planning for the future!

Pompeii Dude
Love, love, love it here. Wish people thousands of years from now could see how awesome it is. If only there was some way to freeze this moment in time . . .

St. Patrick

 St. Patrick
Another fulfilling day tending to the early Irish Christians and combating the heresy of Pelagianism.

 Todd WOOOOOOOOO fuck yeah, man, PARTY!

 Chad Dude, that totally makes me wanna get fucked up. KEGGER!

 Brad St. Patrick FTW! I'm gonna drink till I puke up my balls.

 Corey Right the eff on, man! Green beer green beer green beer LET'S DO THIS!

 Steve i'jm so druink rite now LOL

 St. Patrick
While I appreciate your enthusiasm, perhaps a better way to celebrate would be silent contemplation and prayer.

 Corey EFFIN-A, bro, gettin' shitfaced and shit right the fuck now HERSAY OF Plegasaurus all UP IN THIS BITCH.

Chad ROFL @Corey dude you r sooo wasted.

Corey Dude, where'd that chick go?

 Steve Ralfin' in the shitter. Bro, gonna pass out.

 Todd FUCKIN' PARTY DRINKIN' SHIT—ST. PATRICK's MY BOY!!! DAWG POUND WOLF PACK!

 St. Patrick Um, thanks for your support?

 Corey Bro, saint, dude, don't be a little bitch. R you a li'l bitch? You need a drink.

 Chad Dude, bro, get my man Sant Partick a dirnk.

 Todd DRINK DRINK DRINK DRINK DRINK.

 Steve LOL LOL srsly, St. Patrick, drink up.

 Brad Li'l bitch St. Patrick is a li'l bitch if he don't get FUCKIN' SHITFACED.

 Todd DRINK DRINK DRINK.

 Chad Don't be a pussy dude, drink up.

St. Patrick

Guys, you were right on the money. Sometimes you just have to cut loose with some refreshing adult beverages. Did I ever tell you about the time I drove all the snakes into the sea?

 Corey Dude. Maybe you'd better slow down.

 Todd Um, last call, bro.

 Steve Somebody get my man St. Patrick a coffee.

 Brad *embarrassing*

Chad You are making a fool of yourself.

Crusades Feed

Pope Gregory VIII
Jesus wants us to kill a bunch of people.

Richard the Lionhearted Really?

Pope Gregory VIII Pretty sure.

Phillip II Who should we kill?

Pope Gregory VIII Muslims.

Richard the Lionhearted Do Muslims believe in Jesus?

Pope Gregory VIII They will!

Phillip II LOL

Saladin Hey, we believe in Jesus.

Pope Gregory VIII Not enough!

Saladin I mean, we believe he existed.

 Pope Gregory VIII HERETICS!

 Christians
Goin' ta get Jerusalem back from the Muslims!

 God likes this.

 Muslims
Defendin' Jerusalem from the infidels!

 God also likes this.

 Christians
We will slay many Muslims for you and reclaim Jerusalem, O Lord.

 God Great! Keep up the good work.

 Muslims
We will never stop slaughtering the Christians and defending Jerusalem, O Lord.

 God Fantastic. Terrific stuff.

 Christians ▶ God
Hey, um, we're confused. You're encouraging both of us? Thought you told us to kill the nonbelievers.

 God Uh-huh. That's right. Snap to it.

Muslims ▶ God

And we thought you told US to kill the nonbelievers!

 God Yup. Sure did. Get to work.

 God
LOL

Genghis Khan

 Mongol Hordes invited Genghis Khan to Conquerville

 Genghis Khan I'm pretty busy, you guys.

 Mongol Hordes Come on, you never do anything with us anymore.

 Genghis Khan OK, OK.

Genghis Khan's Conquest of Asia on Conquerville has failed.

 Mongol Hordes You got to spend more time clickin'.

 Genghis Khan Sorry, I guess I got caught up with ACTUALLY CONQUERING ASIA.

👍 **8% of Asian Men with Genghis Khan's DNA** like this.

William Wallace

Andrew Moray
We shall take the Stirling Bridge!

England dislikes this.

 William Wallace Yes!

Andrew Moray
We shall defeat the English!

 William Wallace Right on!

Andrew Moray
We shall lead our forces to victory for all Scots!

 William Wallace What color do we paint our faces?

 Andrew Moray Come again?

 William Wallace We got to look badass, bro!

 Andrew Moray Um, yeah. I think we got to do some planning before the battle.

 William Wallace Duh. We got to color coordinate this.

Andrew Moray

Here's the plan: hold back until half the English pass, then we kill them all as fast as we can. Got it?

William Wallace Monster faces! We'll scare the shit out of 'em by painting our faces up like monster faces!

Andrew Moray Monster faces?

William Wallace Maybe animal faces? Like a cat- or a fox-face? Fox-face! That's it! Oh man, the English'll be all WTF, a fox-man? GET ME OUTTA HERE!!! LOL

Andrew Moray

Um, OK, back to planning. As the English cross the bridge, our forces lie in wait. Now let us assemble our troops for training!

William Wallace I don't know if we're going to have much time for training. Got to paint a lotta scary scary fox-faces.

Andrew Moray A FOX IS NOT SCARY!

William Wallace Then . . . we're going with cat-face?

Andrew Moray Why would you . . . NO!!

William Wallace Dude, you're right. Maybe just paint our faces a fiery red! Attack of the red faces!

Andrew Moray We are heading into battle heavily outnumbered!!

William Wallace Do you think red face will go with my horse? OH SHIT, I GOT IT . . . We paint our HORSES' FACES! Come ridin' down all badass with horse-face look like fox-face!

 Andrew Moray Listen to what you're saying.

 William Wallace The English will be all "Jesus, look at the size of that fox!"

 Andrew Moray

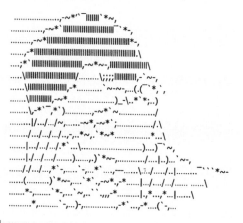

 William Wallace Cool! How did you do that? Can you make his face blue? BLUE! OH SNAP, THAT'S IT!

The Black Plague

Rats and **Fleas** have invited you

I'M INFECTED   MAYBE INFECTED
PLEASE GOD DON'T LET ME BE INFECTED

100 Million
Attending

 30–60% of
Europe

 Those
"Bring Out
Your Dead"
Guys

Not Attending

 Modern
Medical
Knowledge

When	Sometime between Can't-Breathe O'Clock and Face-Boils-Thirty
Where	All Over Your Festering Pustule-Ridden Body
Created By	Lack of Hygiene, Rats and Fleas (but we'll probably blame it on Jews)

 Peasants
Do symptoms include scalding fever, black oozing tumors, and vomiting blood?

 Black Plague Absolutely!

 Peasants Guess I'll have to miss this.

 Black Plague Wrong!

 Peasants You know what? I'll actually be in, um, Russia. Yeah, Russia. Sorry!

 Black Plague Cool! See ya there!

Peasants Actually, I meant Yemen.

 Black Plague Awesome! We'll catch up in Yemen!

 Peasants Take a hint, Black Plague!!

 Priests
Will this plague create a crisis of faith in the Church and God Himself?

The Pope does not like this.

 Black Plague Definitely!

 Priests And since priests and monks help sickies, will we be disproportionately infected?

 Black Plague You got it!

 Priests Looks like I won't be able to make it.

 Black Plague That's really not an option.

Joan of Arc

Joan of Arc
More trippy visions. Guess I have to help France kick England's ass now.

> **France** likes this.
>
> **England** Sez who?
>
> **Joan of Arc** St. Catherine, St. Michael, and St. Margaret.
>
> **England** This war's been going on a hundred years and they decide to chime in now?

Joan of Arc is at the **Siege of Orléans**.

> **France** likes this.
>
> **England** WTF?
>
> **Joan of Arc** In your face!
>
> 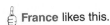 **England** More like in your head! Lucky break, crazy!

Joan of Arc is at the **Battle of Jargeau**.

> **England** Shit!

Joan of Arc is at the **Battle of Beaugency**.

 England FML!

Joan of Arc is at the **Siege of Saint-Pierre-le-Moûtier**.

 England Goddammit!!

 Joan of Arc is granted **nobility**.

 Joan of Arc
You're going down in flames, England!

 England Not sure you got that vision exactly right.

Joan of Arc is captured at the **Siege of Compiègne**.

Joan of Arc is being tried for **Heresy**.

 England likes this.

 Joan of Arc
Is this trial religious or political?

 England Can anyone honestly tell the difference anymore?

 Joan of Arc Bring it!

 England Do you believe you are in the Grace of God?

 Joan of Arc If I am not, may God put me there; and if I am, may God so keep me.

 England Crap, this is gonna be a pain in the ass.

Joan of Arc I have foreseen it.

 England You just need to sign an abjuration and this will all be over.

 Joan of Arc I can't read. What does it say?

 England Different stuff.

Joan of Arc is at **The Stake** with **Burning**.

Christopher Columbus

Christopher Columbus
Off to find a shortcut to the East Indies! Wish me luck!

Queen Isabella Yr awesome.

Christopher Columbus You are! Thx for the boats.

Queen Isabella YW.

Christopher Columbus is in the **Atlantic Ocean** with the **Nina, the Pinta, & the Santa Maria.**

Christopher Columbus This is a shortcut?

Christopher Columbus is in the **West Indies** with a **Bunch of Indians.**

Indigenous Peoples Um, this isn't the East Indies. It's a whole different continent.

Christopher Columbus Who's going to believe a bunch of Indians?

Indigenous Peoples WTF is an Indian?

Amerigo Vespucci Yo, Chris, might actually be a new continent.

 Martin Waldseemüller Lookin' that way.

 Christopher Columbus Even if that's true, which it's not, and I will refuse to believe it until the day I die, but even if it WERE true, I am still the first one to discover it!

 Leif Erikson Um, bro?

 Indigenous Peoples "Indigenous," dawg. Look it up.

Martin Luther

Martin Luther
Just nailed my 95 Theses to the door of the Castle Church in Wittenberg.

Janitor of the Castle Church in Wittenberg COME ON! Seriously? Now I got to putty over the nail hole, repaint the door, repaint the shutters so they match . . NOT COOL.

Catholic Church Plus the heresy.

Martin Luther Maybe I should have nailed them up your butts 'cause that's where your heads are. LOL

Catholic Church Um, what?

Martin Luther So you could see them. With your heads?

Catholic Church You should have nailed them to a pillow because ZZZZZZZZZZZ . . .

Martin Luther 96th Thesis: You're a dick.

Janitor of the Castle Church in Wittenberg Do you know how hard it is to be a janitor in the 1500s? DONT NEED THIS.

Mona Lisa

Mona Lisa changed her profile picture.

 Blue Boy Hawt.

 Girl with a Pearl Earring U r so beautiful.

 The Laughing Cavalier Mrawr!!

 Art Critic Light dances with shadow as Leonardo's dreamscape meets feminine ideal. The mystery is merely a sfumato-fueled duel between the crispness of life and a craggy, fuzzed abstraction; between humanity and nature; between the glowing ooze of woman, the intoxicating fizz of geometry, and the ambiguous musk of sensuality.

Mona Lisa Um, okaaaayyy . . .

 Blue Boy Creepy much?

 Girl with a Pearl Earring U a stalker.

 Leonardo da Vinci Also, the numbers hidden on her eyeballs add up to Jesus had a wife!

Henry VIII

 Henry VIII went from being single to married to **Catherine of Aragon**.

 Henry VIII went from being married to single.

The Pope Do not like.

 Henry VIII went from being single to married to **Anne Boleyn**.

 The Church of England likes this.

The Pope Hey!

Henry VIII went from being married to single.

 Henry VIII went from being single to married to **Jane Seymour**.

The Pope Hope Dr. Quinn has some herbs that'll fix her MISSING HEAD.

 Henry VIII went from being married to single.

 Henry VIII Complications from childbirth. See? Sometimes they just die all natural style. Eff you, Pope!

The Church of England likes this.

The Pope The Church of England doesn't even sound like a real thing.

 Henry VIII went from being single to married to **Anne of Cleves**.

 Henry VIII went from being married to single.

 Henry VIII Didn't kill this one either!

 The Pope Yeah, sometimes you just have your marriages annulled in defiance of God.

 Henry VIII Exactly. IN YOUR FACE.

 Henry VIII went from being single to married to **Catherine Howard**.

 Henry VIII went from being married to single.

Henry VIII Look out, ladies!

 The Pope Seriously.

 Henry VIII went from being single to married to **Catherine Parr**.

Henry VIII Hey, Pope, why weren't you at the wedding? Oh right, because you weren't invited. BURN.

The Pope Hey, if you want to kill your wives, just sit on 'em.

Shakespeare

Shakespeare

Hey, just finished an awesome new play: Two flatulent skateboarding monkeys share an apartment and they DO NOT get along. It's called Macbeth.

Sir Francis Bacon Might need a little work, bro.

Shakespeare Really? Did I mention the monkeys talk?

Shakespeare

OK, then, how about this great new play I just shit out: a bachelor party goes awry when a flatulent hooker steals the best man's houseboat. Callin' it Hamlet.

Christopher Marlowe That doesn't even make sense.

Shakespeare

Just wrote Best. Play. Ever. ROMEO & JULIET: a slobby yet lovable fraternity has to stop their favorite ski resort from being torn down by some mall dudes. Plus there's this girl who's a total dog but then she takes off her glasses and it's like she's real hot. Also her mom is dating their flatulent neighbor who turns out to be a vampire, and then there's a shark, and also everyone battles the yeti who's real powerful because he lives in a haunted house, and then they save the environment.

Edward de Vere, 17th Earl of Oxford Are you sure you're even a writer?

 Shakespeare OK, FINE THEN! You guys are so effin' smart, you write 'em!

Roanoke Colony

John White is **Back in Roanoke Colony** after **3 years**.

 John White
Yo, Roanoke Colony, where u at?

 John White Hallooooooooooo . . .

 John White
??? How could so many just disappear?

 Buffalo Tell me about it.

 Native Americans LOL

 Dinosaurs ROFL @ Buffalo

 Phone Booths And what happens to that one sock in the dryer? Am I right, people?

 Phone Booths In addition to being phone booths, I'm also a stand-up comedian from the '80s.

Sir Walter Raleigh

 Sir Walter Raleigh
I love smoking.

 Europe WTF is smoking?

 Sir Walter Raleigh It's awesome, is what it is.

Sir Walter Raleigh added a photo to his album **Smoking Is Awesome!**

Awesome!!

 Europe That looks ridiculous. Where can I buy a pack?

 Cancer and **Cartoon Camels** like this.

Pilgrims

 Pilgrims
Tired of religious discrimination and feeling unwelcome. Let's go to America and take some land from the godless savages.

 Other Pilgrims If the pagans don't like it, they can leave!

 Pilgrims Let's roll.

The Pilgrims are on the **Mayflower** with **Death**.

 Other Pilgrims
If God didn't want us to make this journey he wouldn't be killing so many of us.

 Pilgrims Man, us pilgrims got Him figured out.

The Pilgrims are at **Plymouth Rock** with **Squanto**.

 Squanto
What's up, guys? Welcome to the neighborhood.

 Pilgrims An Indian who speaks English!

 Other Pilgrims He must be possessed by the devil!

 Pilgrims Kill him!

Squanto Slow yr roll, dawg. I speak English because I was kidnapped by an Englishman to be sold into slavery in Spain but got away and eventually found my way back.

 Pilgrims And you still talk to white people?

 Squanto You can't all be bad, can you?

 Pilgrims Um . . .

The First Thanksgiving

The Pilgrims Who Aren't Dead have invited you

Date	Thanksgiving, you ignorant savages.
Location	Pilgrimtown (formerly Indianburg)
More Info	Having a big dinner to celebrate us not dying during the winter. Indians welcome! For now.

Attending

 Pilgrims

 Our Friends the Red-skinned Heathens

Not Attending

 Turkey and Stuffing 'Cause Instead They Ate Gross Stuff like Clams and Seals

 We're not Kidding. They Ate Seals.

 Squanto
I'll bring maize!

> **Pilgrims** Big surprise, LOL

 Pilgrims
Oh man, I ate too much.

> **Squanto** I'd unbutton my pants if I wore pants, LOL

> **Pilgrims** ROFL

> **Pilgrims** But seriously, put some pants on.

Pocahontas

Pocahontas
OMG, this white guy Daddy's about to kill is so cute!

Captain John Smith *blushes*

Powhatan LOL, looks like my little girl has a crush!

Pocahontas OMG, Daddy, you're embarrassing me on FB!!!

Powhatan Ha, ha. Sorry, princess.

Captain John Smith Little help here?

Pocahontas OMG, Daddy, don't kill him! Give him some corn instead.

Powhatan Whatever you want, sweetie.

Captain John Smith Thanks! And I promise that you will never regret sparing my life and not letting all the white people starve.

Pocahontas OMG, even his empty promises are hawt.

Salem Witch Trials

Mass Hysteria invited you

Location	Salem, Massachusetts
Created By	Religious and Political Leaders Who Are Just Looking Out for the Best Interests of People Who Aren't Witches
More Info	Know a witch? Bring 'em on down! Not sure if they're witches? We'll figure it out for ya!

Attending

 Your Pious, Bloodthirsty Neighbors

 People Afraid of Made-up Stuff

 The Devil! Seriously, He Was Just Over There! And He Looked a Lot Like That Stuck-up Bitch Mary Eastey

Hanging

 Those Who Are Somehow Different from Us or Against Whom We Bear a Grudge

You, if You Don't Watch It

 Villager
Are these real witches or just people you don't like?

 William Stoughton We'll see after the trial!

 Cotton Mather But spoiler alert: real witches.

 Villager What time do you burn the witches?

 William Stoughton No burning. They burn witches in Europe. This is America! We just hang 'em.

 Villager No burning? Not sure if I can make it.

 Townsperson I'm moving back to Europe.

Barbaric Calvinist Can't we burn their bodies after we hang them? Best of both worlds!

 Farmer
My wife cast a spell on me with her constant nagging. Can we put her on trial too?

 Cotton Mather More the merrier!

 Farmer If we run out of time we can just throw her on the fire.

 William Stoughton Once again: no burning. Just hanging. Oh, occasionally maybe we'll crush people under heavy rocks until they confess. But mainly hanging.

 Farmer's Wife Wait a minute. I'm not a witch. My husband's the witch, with his laziness and his not taking out the trash.

 Farmer Oh, here we go . . .

 Cotton Mather You better both come down. We'll find out who the real witch is!

 Cotton Mather Spoiler alert: You're both witches.

George Washington

 George Washington
Fun fact: I don't actually have wooden teeth.

 Colonist SHOW US THE DENTAL RECORDS.

 Patriot And the long-form dental records too! No forgeries that could be cobbled together in any Printmaker's Shoppe or Bindery.

 Colonial Real Estate Mogul Washington's teeth are the greatest scam in history!

 George Washington
I have false teeth; they're just made of gold, ivory, other teeth, etc.

 Patriot I'm no Toother, but I find it interesting he's only now disclosing what his teeth are made of.

 Colonist How long did it take you to come up with that story, George WashingSCUM?

 Colonist
What else are you hiding? Did you even cut down the cherry tree?

 George Washington Um, no, not really.

 Colonist "I CANNOT TELL A LIE" IS A LIE.

George Washington Mythmaking is important in the founding of any nation LOL . . .

 Patriot Did you throw a silver dollar across the Potomac?

 George Washington I mean, that seems like a waste . . .

 Patriot Are you married to Martha?

 George Washington We have . . . an arrangement.

Thomas Jefferson

 Thomas Jefferson went from being married to single.

 Sally Hemings Single? Don't I count?

 Thomas Jefferson Sure! You count as 3/5 of a person. LOL!

 Sally Hemings I mean in your relationship status, smarty-pants.

 Thomas Jefferson is now listed as in 3/5 of a relationship with **Sally Hemings**.

 Thomas Jefferson ROFL

 Sally Hemings Real romantic.

 Thomas Jefferson What do you want from me? I have sex with slaves.

Ben Franklin

Ben Franklin
Early to bed and early to rise, makes a man healthy, wealthy, and wise. Also, sex with prostitutes is fantastic.

Almanac Reader This is mostly great advice.

18th Century Farmwife ?? Really like the part about getting up early—could do without the prostitute stuff.

Ben Franklin
Fish and visitors stink after three days. Also, if you're ever in France, have sex with a prostitute. Two, if possible.

Almanac Reader First part: very funny. Second part seems tacked on and, to be frank, a little offensive.

18th Century Farmwife So true about houseguests! Do not approve of the French whore threesome part.

Ben Franklin
Little strokes fell great oaks. I came up with that one while having sex with a prostitute.

Almanac Reader See, again, I thought that was a great little saying up until the part about the prostitute.

18th Century Farmwife Have to agree that the prostitute stuff seems a little out of left field.

 Ben Franklin Sorry, folks. Need to work on divorcing my folksy wisdom from my perverse sexual appetites.

Paul Revere

Paul Revere ▶ Concord
The British are coming! The British are coming!

Concord Thx, buddy.

Paul Revere What'd we ever do before Facebook?

Paul Revere's Horse I know, right?

Betsy Ross

 Betsy Ross
Go American Revolution! Women are ready to take a stand alongside men and defeat the Redcoats! You'd be surprised what we're capable of! Give us the chance, and we can do anything!

> **George Washington** Can you sew?

> **Betsy Ross** Um, sure, I guess.

> **George Washington** Gonna need a flag to fly over some forts, maybe a few boats. You know how we men like to mark our territory! Ha ha. And I thought, well, I'll ask ol' Betsy, for she's a girl, and that's what girls do. Sew things for men.

> **Betsy Ross** Great.

> **George Washington** So now you be a good little girl and sew a flag for Daddy.

 Betsy Ross
Working on the American flag. Changed the number of points on the stars from six to five.

> **George Washington** Ain't that cute!

Thomas Jefferson Adorable.

 Ben Franklin Why, it seems the feminine mind is capable of making a decision! Especially if it involves one of the few things their intelligence can process, such as cleaning or baking pies or sewing. Great job, honey.

 Betsy Ross *sighs*

 George Washington Don't forget the stripes! Delaware really wants some stripes.

 Betsy Ross I didn't forget the fucking stripes.

 Delaware likes this.

Marie Antoinette

 Marie Antoinette
Let them eat cake.

 Bourgeoisie WTF?

 Peasantry B*tch, you goin' down

 Marie Antoinette You guys, I totally never said that.

 Peasantry It's right up there, dumbass. We got eyes. Poor, breadless eyes.

 Marie Antoinette
Please ignore all posts from me. I got hacked!

 Bourgeoisie You gonna get hacked, all right.

Beethoven

 Archduke Rudolph
YOUR FIFTH SYMPHONY IS AMAZING!

 Beethoven Caps lock is on, friend.

 Prince Kinsky
BEETHOVEN! BEETHOVEN! HEY!
HEEEEEEEEY!

 Beethoven Yes! What?

 Prince Kinsky LOVE THE NINTH!

 Beethoven No need for all caps, bud.

 Prince Lobkowitz
HEY, MAN! DUN-DUN-DUN DUUHHN! YEAH!!!

 Beethoven Why are you shouting at me?

 Prince Lobkowitz AREN'T YOU DEAF?

 Beethoven I'M DEAF BUT I CAN READ.

Prince Lobkowitz You don't have to yell.

 Beethoven Unfriended.

Napoleon

Napoleon
Behold the Facebook of Napoleon, Emperor of France.

Italy Squeeee!!! How kewt!

Napoleon Cute, I am not so sure. Bold and majestic, maybe . . .

Spain *wants to pinch his widdle cheeks*

Napoleon You will do no such thing!

Belgium Awwwww, he's so tiny!

Napoleon I am of average size for a man of this era!

Switzerland Adorable! In his big hat!

Napoleon Perhaps you are mixing up English and French units of measurement?

Netherlands "Can I haz helps 2 climbs on teh pretty ponyzz?"

Napoleon There is no steed that Napoleon cannot mount with ease!

 Germany OMG!! Somebody's throwing the most adorable temper tantrum EVERZ! LOL!

Poland *melts* Such a li'l sweetie with his li'l complex.

 Napoleon You are all in for a severe conquering.

A Fan Page of the Life of David Crockett of the State of Tennessee, Created by Himself.

LIKE

Davy Crockett
Yahoo, America! It's Davy Crockett, the frontiersiest congressman this here US of A ever did see! Thought I'd set up a fan page for all the admirers of my plainspoken, bear-killin' ways. Here's a pic of my hat!

Davy Crockett has posted a pic to his album **Dadgum! What a Hat!.**

Dadgum! What a hat!

Mark A-hole.

Davy Crockett
CrockettQuote of the Day: Be always sure you're right, then go ahead.

Mark You weren't right about that hat but you went ahead anyway.

 Davy Crockett
I been hearin' some scuttlebutt on this here fan page that some fellers ain't rightly smitten with my hat. I say bull hockey! If'n you don't like the hat, you don't like the Davy! Troll much, trolls?

 Mark Your hat looks ridiculous.

 Davy Crockett Just out of curiosity, Mark, you wouldn't happen to be a low-down mangy raccoon, would you?

 Mark No.

 Davy Crockett created a poll. 📈

Do you like my hat?

YES	3%
NO	2%
I'M A RACCOON.	95%

 Davy Crockett Why in blazes would so many dadburned lice-eaten sack-of-mess raccoons be a-takin' a Facebook poll?

 Mark Your hat is an affront to God.

 Davy Crockett
Goldang it, Davy Crockett without his coonskin cap ain't rightly Davy Crockett a-tall. It's like my thing! What else would I even wear?

 Mark sent **Davy Crockett** a link: **Popular Hats of the 19th Century.**

Davy Crockett

You raccoons are a messin' with Davy Crockett's self-confidence. Get offa my fan page!

Mark No idea what you're talking about. Just a lover of backwoods braggin' and men's fashion.

Davy Crockett Fine, then! You raccoons can go to hell, and I'll go to Texas.

Davy Crockett has been invited to the event **the Alamo**.

The Alamo

You were invited by **Mexico**

When	Feb. 23–Mar. 6, 1836
Where	The Free Republic of Texas! Or possibly Mexico.
Creator	The Texas Revolution
Info	The stars at night are big and bright. So are the explosions.

1,600
Attending
1,500 Mexicans

100 Texans

Not
Attending
Pee-Wee's Bike

Davy Crockett
Somebody want to tell me what all these Mexicans are so mad about?

Mark Dunno. Maybe you wore a hat made out of Mexicans?

Sam Houston
Mexico forces us Texans to tithe to the Catholic Church and speak Spanish as the official language. They're tryin' to run us off! Cultural insensitivity and hostility to immigrants? That don't sound like Texas to me!

Slave Owner Don't forget they want to take away slavery! They can have slavery when they pry it from my cold gringo hands.

Santa Anna
You gringos were supposed to settle Texas and grow food for all Mexico, not throw off the yoke of oppressive imperial rule.

Sam Houston You just revolted against Spain.

 Santa Anna I KNOW, BUT YOU GUYS JUST GOT HERE. GIVE US A BREAK; WE'RE EXHAUSTED.

 Santa Anna
Siege time, a-holes.

 Davy Crockett Man, that's a lot of Mexicans.

 Sam Houston With you in spirit, boys. Sorry I can't be there. I got a thing.

 Jim Bowie I'm sick in bed. Somebody hand me my knife.

 Davy Crockett Srsly, that's a lot of Mexicans.

 William B. Travis I ain't seen that many Mexicans since last Tuesday.

 Jim Bowie What's last Tuesday?

 William B. Travis That's when I had my yardwork d— OW I AM SHOT!

 Davy Crockett
Um . . . are some of them Mexicans actually raccoons?

 Mark No.

James W. Marshall

James W. Marshall
What luck! Found some gold today!

49ers Rly? Where?

James W. Marshall Oh, out in California.

49ers Specifically.

James W. Marshall Um . . . Sutter's Mill. Why?

49ers No reason. See ya soon.

Everybody has been invited to **the Gold Rush**

James W. Marshall Dang it.

Pony Express

Pony Express Rider

Going on a run right now! Gettin' mail from Missouri to California in just 10 days!

 California Amazing! You have revolutionized communication!

 Missouri Why, it's like me talking to you right now but with only a 10-day lag.

 California FB me when you get here.

Pony Express Rider

Attacked by Indians in Kansas. Mail's OK, tho.

 California Close one! Those savages could have completely severed our line of communication!

Missouri How would we have kept in touch?

Pony Express Rider

Horse gave out. I'm tuckered too. Gotta keep movin'.

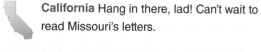 **California** Hang in there, lad! Can't wait to read Missouri's letters.

 Missouri Can't wait for you to read them!

 California What do you say in them?

Missouri Not much. Normal stuff.

 California Do you describe the weather?

 Missouri Oh, yes. The weather's been great.

 California Can't wait to read all about it!

 Pony Express Rider
Another Indian attack. Mouth full of dust. Whole body aches from these brutal rides.

 California What else do you say in your letters?

 Missouri I hate to ruin the surprise.

 California Let me guess.

 Missouri Oh, do!

 California What fun!

 Pony Express Rider Question—why am I riskin' my durn neck to carry letters across the dang country when you're already talkin' to each other on Facebook?

California Do you update me on the progress of your vegetable garden?

Missouri The tomatoes are coming in nicely!

 California Spoiler Alert!

 Missouri LOL

 California LOL

 Pony Express Rider Jesus Christ.

 Pony Express Rider I swear to God, if y'all talk about this kind of meaningless crap in your letters—

 California No, no! Letters are for posterity.

 Missouri The written word lends immortality to even the smallest of musings.

 California The very effort of physically writing words causes the author to reconsider, adjust, and better their notions.

 Missouri Facebook is like, who gives a shit.

 California You're bored at work or something.

Missouri LOL

California LOL

Abraham Lincoln

Abraham Lincoln ▶ Slaves
Guess what?

Slaves What?

Abraham Lincoln You're free.

Slaves GTFO!

Abraham Lincoln Yup. Just freed ya.

Slaves Thanks!

Abraham Lincoln Yr welcome.

Slaves ▶ Abraham Lincoln
Oh, one more thing. By "free," do you mean equal?

Abraham Lincoln Well . . .

Slaves Safe from angry white mobs?

Slaves Assured our rightful place in American society?

Slaves Welcome in any job or restaurant or neighborhood, working and dining and living side by side with whites?

 Abraham Lincoln Um, look at the time. I got a play to get to!

 The South
See? Knew all along that Lincoln was an abolitionist!

 Abraham Lincoln Well, at one point I encouraged freed slaves to resettle in Liberia.

 Slaves Where's Liberia?

 Abraham Lincoln Um, Africa.

 Slaves Hold up. You wanted to SEND US BACK TO AFRICA?!?

 Abraham Lincoln Seriously, we'll talk about this when I get back from the play.

Harriet Tubman

Slave
PM me how I can get tickets for the Underground Railroad.

Runaway Slave
It'd be awesome if you could post the schedule for the Underground Railroad. I'm planning on escaping around 9-ish and don't want to miss my train.

Escaped Slave
If the train is underground, how do we breathe?

Fugitive Slave
Do you have any trains that aren't underground? I'm claustrophobic.

Runaway Slave Being underground doesn't bother me, but I've always been scared of trains.

Fugitive Slave LOL Ain't we a pair.

Runaway Slave LOL

Slave Owner
You slaves sure are dumb. You actually think some underground train will carry you to freedom? LOL! Why, we got men all over the South with shovels and pickaxes. We ain't gonna quit diggin' until we find that train, no matter how deep underground it is. Try to put one over on white people, will ya?

 Harriet Tubman likes this.

Chinese Railroad Worker
Where I get job work on underground railroad? That way when I die I already buried.

Some White Lady
I am not an escaped slave; however, I am planning a vacation in the next couple of weeks and my kids would love a trip on the Underground Railroad! All they talk about are trains and gophers.

Harriet Tubman joined the group "**I f#$%king hate people.**"

News Feed

 H. M. Stanley ▶ David Livingstone
Dr. Livingstone, I presume?

 David Livingstone OH HAI.

Aussie Feed

 England
Man, have we got a lot of convicts! We're running out of room!

 America Don't send 'em here, LOL

 England
Looking to ship our convicts somewhere desolate, deserted, nobody around . . . like Australia!

 Aborigines Um . . .

 Aborigines Guys? We, like, live here and stuff.

 England At last we can get rid of all our criminals and rapists and sociopaths.

 Kangaroos Oh noes . . .

 English Convicts just checked in at **Australia**

 England ▶ English Convicts
You sit here and think about what you've done.

 English Convicts No worries, mate.

 **England** ???

 English Convicts That's how we talk now.

Billy the Kid

Billy the Kid
I done killed 21 men!

Cattle Rancher Yeah, right.

Posse Member Where? In your mommy's basement? LOL!

Billy the Kid
I'm a wanted man!

Cattle Rancher Who's looking for you? Your babysitter? LOL

Billy the Kid
I'm a ruthless killer!!!!

Posse Member Does he want his blankie? LOL!

Billy the Kid
Keep it up, I'll kill YOU!

Cattle Rancher Cyberbullying is a crime!

Pat Garrett Sure is.

Posse Member Do your parents know you're using the computer?

Billy the Kid
I SHOOT PEOPLE IN COLD BLOOD!! I DON'T CARE 'BOUT NO LAWS!

 Posse Member I just don't understand the youth these days. Is threatening murder supposed to be cute? You ought to be ashamed of yourself.

 Billy the Kid I'll shoot you down dead in the street!

 Cattle Rancher Grow up.

Vincent van Gogh

Vincent van Gogh has joined the group **One-Eared People**

Paul Gauguin
Ears to you! LOL!

Paul Gauguin Get it? "EARS" to you? ROTFLMFAO!

Vincent van Gogh What?

Arthur Conan Doyle

Arthur Conan Doyle
Please become a fan of my latest book! Just getting started, but it's gonna be a good one!
The Adventures of Sherlock Holmes, World's Greatest Plumber

Page: 0 people are fans.

Arthur Conan Doyle
OK, I get it. Nobody likes it because it's about a plumber! Who wants to read about a plumber? So please become a fan of my NEW book!
The Adventures of Sherlock Holmes, World's Greatest Ventriloquist

Page: 0 people are fans.

Arthur Conan Doyle LOL Back to the drawing board!

Arthur Conan Doyle
I dare you not to like this one!
The Adventures of Sherlock Holmes, World's Greatest Horse Doctor

Page: 0 people are fans.

I. K. Funk A horse doctor is called a veterinarian.

Arthur Conan Doyle I KNOW WHAT A GODDAM VETERINARIAN IS!

Arthur Conan Doyle
The Adventures of Sherlock Holmes, World's Greatest Siamese Twins

Page: 0 people are fans.

Arthur Conan Doyle
The Adventures of Sherlock Holmes, World's Greatest Granddad

Page: 0 people are fans.

Arthur Conan Doyle
The Adventures of Sherlock Holmes, World's Greatest Werewolf

Page: 0 people are fans.

 Arthur Conan Doyle Eff all you guys.

Arthur Conan Doyle
OK, think I got it now! This is it! You guys are going to fan this page so hard!
The Adventures of Sherlock Holmes, World's Greatest Detective

Page: 0 people are fans.

 Arthur Conan Doyle Come on, you guys! How can it get better than that?!

 I. K. Funk Don't like the name.

Arthur Conan Doyle
The Adventures of the World's Greatest Detective, Columbo

Page: 800 kajillion people are fans.

 Arthur Conan Doyle Nailed it.

Jack the Ripper

Lives in **Whitechapel, London, England**

Beliefs and Values

Quotes
"It cuts like a knife, but it feels so right."
—Bryan Adams

Favorites

Movies   Pretty Woman, Klute, Milk Money
Music   Slayer, Shonen Knife, Bobby Darin

Activities and Interests

Activities   Table Tennis, Cricket, Murdering Prostitutes
Interests   Anatomy, Cutlery, Correspondence, Dark
                Alleys, Leather Aprons, Preserved Kidneys

Basic Information

About Jack   Just your average, everyday member of
                royalty or maybe a doctor or maybe a
                schoolmaster or maybe a barber or maybe
                a bootmaker or maybe a journalist or maybe
                a fish porter or perhaps a cotton merchant
                or a Freemason.

Contact Information

If you're a whore in Whitechapel, I'll get in touch with you.

Mark Twain

Mark Twain
Just finished my memoirs!

Reader Can't wait to read 'em!

Mark Twain Coming 2010.

Fan Um, what?

Mark Twain This book was written exclusively for future people.

Reader What the hell, man? No way to treat your fans.

Mark Twain Only future people, with their flying automobiles and laser pistols, are worthy of my recollections.

Fan I can't believe this!

Mark Twain Of course you can't. Only future men with their humongous, blue-veined future brains could comprehend my trials and tribulations and ruminations on the Spanish-American War.

Reader You suck!

Mark Twain The future is the only place that can hold my thoughts. A civilized future, in which we have colonized Mars and turned its alien inhabitants into our slaves. Tiny green men will wait on us hand and foot. They will read my autobiography aloud to their human masters in a tongue only future men shall understand.

 Reader If you love 'em so much, why don't you go talk to your Facebook fans from the stupid future?

 Mark Twain Facebook's grotesque system of insipid time wasting, oafish nattering, and wholesale larceny of private information is much more suited to the illiterate, malodorous clod of today, not the erudite and winsome denizen of the 21st century who smells like cake.

 Fan I hope your precious future people ban your stupid books.

 Mark Twain YOU WATCH YOUR MOUTH ABOUT FUTURE PEOPLE!

George Washington Carver

 George Washington Carver
Did you know that peanuts can be made into dyes for cloth or leather?

 746 people like this.

 Poor Farmers Amazing!

 The South Very helpful.

 Tuskegee Institute Peanuts FTW!

 George Washington Carver
You can also make a fine axle grease out of peanuts.

 189 people like this.

 The South Nice.

 Poor Farmers You don't say.

 Tuskegee Institute Huh.

George Washington Carver

Peanuts make an excellent face cream or lotion.

 16 people like this.

George Washington Carver

Peanuts make a terrific tannic acid!

 2 people like this.

George Washington Carver

Peanuts can be turned into milks or vinegars.

 0 people like this.

 Poor Farmers OK, peanuts, I get it!

 **The South** Stop spamming me with peanuts, peanuts, peanuts!

 Tuskegee Institute Next time my Feed is clogged with you talking about peanuts I'm dropping you off FB!

 George Washington Carver likes **Peanuts**.

Tuskegee Institute No shit.

Wilbur Wright

Wilbur Wright
Traveling to the location of our manned gliding experiment. Chose Kitty Hawk, NC, because its conditions were the most suitable: breeze off the Atlantic coast, soft, sandy landing surfaces.

> **Orville Wright** ROAD TRIP!!!! The Wright Brothers are BACK, baby!!!!!

Wilbur Wright
I find Kitty Hawk to be perfect. It is remote and provides privacy from reporters.

> **Orville Wright** This place sucks. Where are the babes?

Wilbur Wright
We shall set upon our first experiment at dawn. I am optimistic concerning this unmanned kite.

> **Orville Wright** How the hell am I gonna get laid here? There's not even a decent sports bar.

Wilbur Wright
Experiment was not altogether a success—wing-warping created differential drag at the wingtips.

> **Orville Wright** Also unsuccessful: my snatch run. Kitty Hawk must be full of lesbians or something. Get me out of here!

Wilbur Wright
Have perfected the movable vertical rudder! Now must contact various engine manufacturers.

Orville Wright How about we contact Greyhound and get the eff out of here? I hear there's a good tittie bar in Virginia Beach.

 Wilbur Wright
Cannot find an engine that is sufficiently lightweight. Will ask our good friend and mechanic Charlie Taylor. Perhaps he could build such an engine.

 Charlie Taylor likes this.

 Orville Wright Charlie, DO NOT come here! I'll get back to Dayton to pick it up! THERE IS NO PUSSY TO BE HAD AT KITTY HAWK!!

 Charlie Taylor Screw that, then.

 Wilbur Wright
Charlie built an engine in just six weeks! To keep the weight low enough, the engine block was cast from aluminum.

 Orville Wright Do you know how many times I've masturbated since we've been here? 1,263 times. 1,264, here I come.

 Wilbur Wright posted a pic.

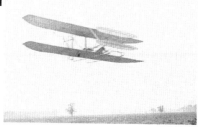

As you can see we were successful today making the first controlled, powered, and sustained heavier-than-air human flight!

 Orville Wright Hurrah! Mankind has achieved flight! So I presume it is now possible to fly me the HELL OUTTA KITTY HAWK!

Typhoid Mary

Future Typhoid Victim
Love your cooking!

Typhoid Mary Thanks so much!

Future Typhoid Victim BTW, how'd you get that name?

Typhoid Mary IDK . . . guess my parents just liked the name Mary.

Future Typhoid Victim LOL!!! Don't feel so good.

Albert Einstein

Albert Einstein has joined **Facebook**.

Science
Hey, you're the smartest guy alive. Why're you wasting time on Facebook?

Albert Einstein Wut you smokin', cuz? Facebook is rad! I can holla at my bros, peep on a hawtie's pics, play Farmville or the gangster one, be all "I like this!" or "I poked you!" and shizz. It's only like the greatest thing ever.

Science Are you sure you're smart?

Albert Einstein $E = mc^2$, bitchezz.

Titanic

 Titanic
I'm unsinkable.

 Iceberg Sunk ya!

 Titanic FML.

 Iceberg Nature 1, Man 0.

 Titanic We'll get you back with global warming.

 Iceberg Drink up, mofo!

 Polar bears like this.

 Titanic
Women and children first!

 Men You know, chivalry has its place. I'm the first one to hold a door for a lady or compliment her hat. But I'm thinking, you know, this is the 20th century, equality, etc. Perhaps men and women are not so different after all.

 Titanic Are you saying you want on the lifeboat?

Men Dear God, yes.

 Titanic What about the children? You would kick them off and send them to a frigid, watery grave?

 Men They are Irish.

 Titanic Oh, then, by all means.

 Titanic
Going down.

 Captain Right behind you.

 Titanic After you, then.

 Captain No, please, after you.

 Titanic I insist!

 Captain Shall we go down together?

 Titanic Lovely.

 Captain Near, far, wherever you are . . .

Titanic LOL

 **Captain** My heart will go on . . .

 Titanic Not after hypothermia sets in!

It's a Long Way to News Feed-erary

 The Great War
Archduke Franz Ferdinand of Austria has been assassinated in Sarajevo! Looks like I'm about to start!!

 Franz Ferdinand Nope, they missed . . . Got the poor bastards in the car behind me. On my way now to visit to visit 'em in the hospital.

 The Black Hand Which route you takin'?

 Franz Ferdinand Goin' down by the river. Close to the Latin Bridge?

 Gavrilo Princip likes this.

 The Great War
Archduke Franz Ferdinand of Austria has been assassinated in Sarajevo! Looks like I'm about to start!!

 Franz Ferdinand I'm really dead this time.

 Newspapers of the Time
WAR? TENSIONS MOUNT OVER NOBODY MURDERED BY WHO? IN ROCKY BACKWATER HELLHOLE?

The Great War ▶ Europe
Come on, you guys! Let's get it on. War! War! War!

Austria Franz Ferdinand is . . . which one was he again?

The Great War Jeez! He was archduke of you! You better invade Serbia!

Austria I guess . . .

Russia Is Serbia the same as Bosnia?

Germany What exactly is Prussia?

The Great War Doesn't matter! WAR! WAR! WAR!

The Great War has **Begun.**

The Great War Awesome sauce! Who wants in on this? Everybody's doin' it!

Rest of Europe Okey-doke!

Newspapers of the Time
WAR! READY-TO-CRUMBLE EMPIRES & PERPLEXING OUTDATED ALLIANCES EQUAL LET'S KILL EVERYBODY!

The Great War ▶ Germany
Rad helmets. All pointy and shit. Nice!

Germany Our helmets are extremely heavy.

Germany has sunk the **Lusitania**.

 Woodrow Wilson This war is none of America's business.

 Teddy Roosevelt Balderdash! IMO.

Germany has sunk **seven U.S. merchant ships**.

 Woodrow Wilson Goddammit.

 Teddy Roosevelt Let's go, pussy.

 The Great War LOL

USA has joined **the Great War**.

 The Great War Now it's a party! A bloody, limb-severing party.

 The Great War likes **Trenches** and **Gas**.

 The Great War Now that's what I call killin'!

Snoopy has shot down the **Red Baron**.

 Marcie likes this.

 Newspapers of the Time
WAR ENDS! WORLD ALL "WTF JUST HAPPENED??"

 Allies Guess we taught Germany a long-lasting lesson!

The Great War
Dudes, this has been a blast! At least I'm going out knowing I'm the greatest war of all time!

 World War II *snickers*

The Twenties

Flappers
The Twenties are the cat's pajamas!

The Cat's Pajamas I am a popular saying in the twenties! I mean something is very good.

Prohibition
Keep on roarin', Twenties! You're when booze is illegal!

 Al Capone likes this.

Drunken Scofflaws And delicious!

Booze People still make me in bathtubs!

Bathtub I am filled with yummy homemade liquor!

Handsome Gadabout
Yo Twenties, you sure are swell! The Great War has ended and I have an automobile.

Hemlines I'm rising!

Handsome Gadabout So am I!

Hemlines LOL

 Handsome Gadabout Seriously, social mores are loosening.

 The Great Gatsby
Sup, Twenties! I'm synonymous with you.

 F. Scott Fitzgerald I moved to Paris!

 Ernest Hemingway C U at the café . . .

 Expatriates Oui! Oui! LOL

 Jazz
Thanks for my popularity during you! I'm like yr soundtrack or something.

 Harlem And thx for my renaissance!

 The Charleston
Dear 20s, luv u! U r when people dance me.

 The Lindy Hop Me too! LOL

 The Jazz Singer
Can u hear me now?

 Steamboat Willie ROFLMAO

Stock Market Crash
I'm ending you, bee-yotch!

 The Great Depression Brother, can u spare a dime?

The Twenties dislike.

Babe Ruth

 Sick Kid
Hey, Babe, can I ask you a favor? Sure would mean a lot to a sick little kid like me.

 Babe Ruth Sure, Kid! You name it!

 Sick Kid Well, the big game's coming up and, I don't know, if you could—never mind.

 Babe Ruth Heh-heh. Don't be shy. Go ahead and ask. Although I think I got a pretty good idea what you want, LOL

 Sick Kid Could you lose a few pounds for me?

 Babe Ruth Say what?

 Sick Kid Take it from someone who's had health problems all his young life. Will you start watching your weight? For me?

 Babe Ruth Sure you don't want me to knock you a couple homers instead?

 Sick Kid Your health is all you got.

 Babe Ruth Right right, sure. I'll look into it.

Sick Kid posted a **link** on **Babe Ruth's** Wall: **List of Major Health Problems Linked to Obesity**.

 Babe Ruth Um, thanks. Def. something to think about.

 Sick Kid

How about the drinking? Alcoholism is a proven contributor to several major health conditions.

 Babe Ruth You know, I could say, "This one's for Johnny" or whatever your name is, and you could listen on the radio, and I'll just clobber that ball, and all the nurses will throw you a party.

 Sick Kid If you don't take care of you, who will?

 Babe Ruth No, I know, but it's just home runs are easier.

 Sick Kid *cough cough*

 Babe Ruth OK, I'll try to make some changes.

 Sick Kid One day at a time.

 Sick Kid

Or how about cutting out the womanizing? Venereal disease is a killer.

 Babe Ruth Jesus Christ, kid. I mean, come on!

 Sick Kid I'm so sick, though.

Babe Ruth How about I just write you a check for $3,000?

👍 **Sick Kid** likes this.

Scopes Monkey Trial

You were invited by **The State of Tennessee**

When	1925
Where	Dayton, TN
Creators	The Butler Act
Info	Bring your own fan, sense of outrage/condescension

Attending
National Press

Religious Zealots

Sweat-Stained Lookee Loos

Maybe Attending
Scientific Awakening

The Holy Spirit

Not Attending
H. G. Wells

Actual Monkeys

 John Scopes
Awesome lesson plan for tomorrow. Hint: hope you like monkeys!

 ACLU likes this.

 State of Tennessee See you in court!

 Judge John T. Raulston
I will be as impartial a judge as I can possibly be without damning myself to Hell.

 Clarence Darrow
Man came from Monkeys.

 William Jennings Bryan Nuh-uh, God made 'em.

 Clarence Darrow You're a moron.

William Jennings Bryan You hate Jesus.

 Monkey I'm ashamed to be your ancestor.

 Clarence Darrow
Scientists testifyin' tomorrow. Sweet.

 Judge John T. Raulston That sounds boring. Overruled.

 William Jennings Bryan Amen.

 Judge John T. Raulston Amen.

 Clarence Darrow Hey, wait!

 Jury
This heah jury finds the little ol' defendant guilty, y'all.

 Judge John T. Raulston Pay up, dude.

 Clarence Darrow See you in Tennessee Supreme Court!

 Tennessee Supreme Court Technicality! Throwin' this shit out. And because it's so fridiculous, we ain't sending it back to a lower court. Screw it.

 Clarence Darrow Dang.

William Jennings Bryan I died 10 days after the trial following a heavy meal.

 Clarence Darrow Amen.

 Public Opinion

But without a court ruling, how will we ever know if evolution is fact? Could it be true? Did man descend from monkeys?

 Monkey I hope to God not.

Bill W.

 Bill W.
Hey, got a great new way to get people sober.

 Drunk Really?

 Bill W It's called Alcoholics Anonymous! We sit in a room, smoke cigarettes, drink stale coffee, and bitch about our lives.

 Alcoholic That sounds terrible.

 Drunk I'd rather drink.

 Barfly Replace stale coffee with lots of vodka and that's pretty much my life right now.

Gandhi

Gandhi posted a photo.
Lunch today!

Gandhi posted a photo.
Had to take a pic of today's scrumptious lunch!

Gandhi posted a photo.
Om nom nom!

 **England** OK, we get it.

FDR

FDR
Hypothetically, if the president couldn't walk, that'd be no big deal, right?

Public No way! If the president can't move his legs, how can he kick Hitler's ass?

Press We're glad you can walk, Mr. President! *winks*

Republicans Depends. Is he also a socialist?

Unemployed I'll carry him around on my shoulders if it pays.

 The Works Progress Administration likes this.

FDR
Just for conversation's sake, if someone was in a wheelchair, say—and I'm just pulling this out of the air here—say it was the president, he should keep the wheelchair out of sight and struggle to the podium with heavy braces and a monster walk to sell the public on the facade of his vigor, right?

Press Absolutely! And we're happy to help brace up this "fictional" prez.

Republicans Are you leading up to taking rich people's wheelchairs and giving 'em to poor people? Because eff them.

Public Wheelchairs, funny walks, whatever. Anything to distract us from the Depression and war.

 FDR posted a poll. 📈

Do you think Imaginary paralyzed presidents are:

AWESOME! SHOWS HE CAN OVERCOME HARDSHIP.	31%
INSPIRING! GREAT MESSAGE TO SEND TO AMERICANS STRUGGLING TO OVERCOME THEIR OWN PROBLEMS.	30%
GROSS! LIMP LEGS BELONG IN WHEELCHAIRS, NOT PRESIDENT CHAIRS.	38%

News Feed

👍 **Germany** likes **Hitler**.

👍 **Jews** like **Oh Fuck**.

👍 **Hitler** likes **Poland**.

👍 **Neville Chamberlain** appeases **Hitler**.

👍 **Neville Chamberlain** appeases **People Who Want Him to GTFO**.

👍 **King George VI** likes **Winston Churchill**.

👍 **France** likes **Surrendering**.

USA dislikes Foreign Wars.

👍 **Japan** likes **Sneak Attacks**.

👍 **USA** likes **Foreign Wars**.

👍 **Russia** likes **Russia**.

👍 **The French Resistance** likes **Seriously, the French Resistance Was a Real Thing**.

👍 **USA** likes **D-day**.

👍 **Hitler** likes **Bunkers**.

👍 **Truman** likes the **H-bomb**.

👍 **Japan** likes **Surrendering**.

👍 **Sailors** like **Kissing Nurses**.

Laika

Laika
I, Laika, will be first dog in space!

 USSR likes this.

Laika
When I return I will be great hero dog! Everyone will want to pet my courageous fur! I will be awarded all the doggy treats I can eat!

 Oleg Gazenko Good dog!

 Laika Thank you, master! I know I will be victorious in glorious mission! I have utmost confidence in infallible Soviet space program and know you have taken every precaution to ensure Laika's safety. I thank you, comrade.

 Oleg Gazenko Um, sure.

Baker
Good luck, Laika! I'll be right behind ya!

 USA likes this.

 Laika SILENCE, capitalist monkey!! USA shall fail! Never send a monkey to do a dog's job!

 Baker I can't wait to eat a space banana!

Laika FOOL! There are no bananas in space!!

 Oleg Gazenko Good dog! You are correct! There is nothing in space. Outer space is a near perfect vacuum.

 Laika Vacuum?

 Oleg Gazenko Yes, comrade.

 Baker I will climb high up in the space trees!

 Laika YOU IMBECILE!! STUPID MONKEY!!!! @Oleg Just how loud is this space vacuum?

 Baker Laika's scared of vacuums!

 Laika ENOUGH, MONKEY! I am hero dog! Scared of nothing!!!! If Laika barks at running vacuum, is not out of fear! Laika has sensitive ears, is all.

 Oleg Gazenko It is not that kind of vacuum, Comrade Dog. Sound cannot travel in space.

 Laika Of course not! Laika knew that.

 Baker
I hope we can be astronaut friends when we return to earth!

 Laika WE WILL NEVER BE FRIENDS, IDIOT MONKEY! I will be far too busy being groomed and walked when I return a hero unto Mother Russia!

Oleg Gazenko Ummmmmm, let us not count our chickens before they are hatched.

 Laika Chickens! Laika hates chickens! Even more than vacuums!

 Baker When I get to space I'm going to meet a Space Chicken!

 Laika SILENCE, MONKEY.

J. Edgar Hoover

Work and Education

Employer Federal Bureau of Investigation (1935–for life)

Beliefs and Values

Religion Conduct surveillance on 'em all and let God sort 'em out.

Politics Whichever guy I got the goods on.

Quotes "I feel pretty, oh so pretty." —Maria, West Side Story

Favorites

Movies Bromances

TV The FBI

Music Theme from The FBI, Judy Garland

Hobbies and Pastimes

Fashion, Surveillance, Destroying Lives

Basic Information

Love Status In a strictly buddy-buddy relationship with **Clyde Tolson**

About J. Edgar Classy broad

John F. Kennedy

 Marilyn Monroe
sings in sultry whisper Happy birthday to
you, happy birthday to you, happy birthday, Mr.
President, happy birthday to you.

> **John F. Kennedy** Thanks! From now on
> why don't you PM me?

> **Bobby Kennedy** Me too!

 Lee Harvey Oswald
Happy birthday!

> **John F. Kennedy** Thanks. Who are you
> again?

> **Lee Harvey Oswald** Oh, just a patsy.

 Fidel Castro
Happy birthday, you capitalist swine. Remember
the Bay of Pigs? LOL!

> **John F. Kennedy** LMFAO!! Always got to
> embarrass me with those old stories on
> my b-day.

 Che Guevara
Happy Birthday! Hope you got the T-shirt.

 Nikita Khrushchev
We will bury you! Also happy birthday.

Richard Nixon
I'm sure you got everything you wanted for your birthday, so no need for Dick Nixon to get you anything . . . rich boy!

Joseph P. Kennedy
Happy Birthday, son! You'll never measure up.

Jackie Kennedy
sings in sultry whisper Happy birthday to you, happy birthday to you—

John F. Kennedy Give it a rest.

Woodstock

You were invited by the **Sixties**

When	Friday, August 15–Monday, August 18, 1969
Where	Some dude's farm
Creators	Filthy Hippies
Info	Cameras will be present, so don't wear anything to embarrass yourself. Tickets mandatory!!

500,000 Attending

 Rain

 Bad Trips

 People Who Aren't Going but Will Say They Were There Anyway

Maybe Attending

 Governor Nelson Rockefeller

 10,000 NY Nat'l Guardsmen

Not Attending

 Dylan

 Nixon

 Sinatra

 Self-Obsessed Baby Boomer
I'll be there! And I'll never let you forget it.

 Oliver Stone likes this.

 John Lennon
Dude, I can totally get the Beatles to show up. Just give Yoko some stage time and I'll make it happen!

 Gonorrhea
I'll be there!

 Shoes Not me!

 Deodorant Me neither! *frownz*

Unattractive Naked Breasts
Can't wait to hang out!

Droopy Mud-Covered Balls likes this.

Brown Acid

Don't take me! lolzzzz

John Lennon

Seriously. I will get the Beatles to perform live for the first time in years. All you have to do is give Yoko some stage time. Twenty minutes, even!

 Yoko Ono likes this.

The Rolling Stones

Little concerned about the security.

 The Hell's Angels like this.

Joni Mitchell

Sorry, doing The Dick Cavett Show instead.

 Dick Cavett likes this

 Joni Mitchell My manager says forty years from now everybody will still be talking about this episode of The Dick Cavett Show.

Dick Cavett believes this.

Ravi Shankar

I'll be there, and so will my trusty sitar, Lucille.

John Lennon

Maybe I didn't make myself clear. Beatles. John. Paul. George. Even Ringo. At Woodstock. History in the f'in making. Just give Yoko ten f'in minutes and I can guarantee you the greatest fucking show ever.

 Yoko Ono Eee! Eee! Eee! Yaeee!

Sha Na Na

In the future, when people think Woodstock, they'll think Sha Na Na.

 John Lennon Seriously? F'in Sha Na f'in Na, and you don't have five f'in minutes for Yoko? You idiots don't deserve the f'in Beatles. F you and your cow pasture.

 Ringo Starr I could probably still make it.

Elvis

Work and Education

Occupation   King

Employers   Bureau of Narcotics and Dangerous Drugs
(1970–present)

Beliefs and Values

Religion   I like to sing gospel songs when I ain't too high.

Politics   American Trilogy Party

Quotes   "Red, get me a sandwich."—me
"Here's your sandwich, E."—Red

Favorites

Movies   Ones where I drive race cars

TV   Shows I ain't shot at yet

Sandwiches   Fried peanut butter and banana

Hobbies and Pastimes

Karate, Buyin' People Cadillacs, Quaaludes, 14-year-old girls (just friends!), 21-year-old girls (wives), Sandwiches (fried peanut butter and banana)

Basic Information

Love Status   'Scilla!

About Elvis   Hungry. Red, get me a sandwich!

Contact Information

Return to Sender. LOL! So high. WHERE'S THAT SANDWICH?

Patty Hearst

Patty Hearst has joined the group **Symbionese Liberation Army**

 The Stockholm Syndrome likes this

 Patty Hearst has changed her name to **Tania**.

Tania just checked in at **Hibernia Bank**.

Tania posted a new pic to her album **Security Cam Photos**.

SLA FTW!!

 Tania
Loving my new job as bank robber, I mean urban guerrilla.

 Brainwashing likes this.

 FBI BUSTED!!!!!

Tania has changed her name back to **Patty Hearst**.

Patty Hearst has been sentenced 35 years for bank robbery.

 Patty Hearst WTF?!!? Uh, brainwashing, hello?!?

 Brainwashing Hello! You're getting very very sleepy . . .

 Patty Hearst I'm not falling for that again!

 Patty Hearst has received the **Executive Grant of Clemency** from **Jimmy Carter**.

 Jimmy Carter I think you've learned your lesson not to rob banks or be brainwashed anymore. You're now free to go act in John Waters movies.

 Serial Mom likes this.

David Berkowitz

 Harvey
Yo, Dave! Got a favor to ask.

 David Berkowitz Beg your pardon?

 Harvey Kill people.

 David Berkowitz Why the hell would I do that?

 Harvey I'm your neighbor's dog! I wouldn't steer you wrong.

 David Berkowitz I guess.

 Harvey Also, when you get done killing some folks, could you bring me a box of Milk-Bones? It's the chewing-food I like and need!

 David Berkowitz CANT GET YOUR VOICE OUT OF MY HEAD.

 Harvey Then you'd better snap to it, yo.

 David Berkowitz Yes, my master.

Harvey Milk-Bones FTW!

 David Berkowitz
Master, I have served you well. You will not be disappointed.

 Harvey Awesome, Dave! Thanks, man! Except I gotta ask you for another solid.

 David Berkowitz I am only here but to obey your commands.

 Harvey OK, one: I need you to kill some more folks for me, and two: if you could get me one of those little rubber toys in the shape of a fire hydrant? They make squeaky sounds when you chew 'em? THEY. ARE. AWESOME!!!

 David Berkowitz You will be pleased, O Master.

 Harvey Score!!!

 David Berkowitz
I have made it so, O Demon Dog of Hell, my master, whom I long to serve.

 Harvey U da man, Dave!

 David Berkowitz If I was not powerless against the ancient demon that has taken your soul and controls my every move, I would most certainly lay waste to your evil existence.

 Harvey Uh-huh. OK, now I need you to bring me some of that dogs-don't-know-it's-not-bacon stuff. I mean, I totally know it's not bacon, but it's got its own thing going on, right? Oh, plus I need you to kill some more people.

Police
What's going on here?

 David Berkowitz This dog's makin' me kill people!

 Harvey Arf arf.

 Police Uh-huh.

 David Berkowitz You have to believe me!

 Harvey Bow-wow.

 Police OK, buddy, you're under arrest.

 David Berkowitz But—he was just—I swear that he—

 Police *pets dog* Good boy.

 Harvey Muah-ha-ha!

King Tut

King Tut
Man! DC was awesome! Gonna have to catch some z's on the way thru to Chi-town! Life on the road is crazy. WINNING.

King Tut
CHICAGO! CHICAGO!! My kinda town? You bet your azz!! Ain't no groupies like Chi-town groupies! Need to save some strength for New Orleans.

King Tut is at the **New Orleans Museum of Art**.

King Tut
Fans lined up around the block. I'm truly humbled. You guys made this happen. If it weren't for you they'd have never dug me up. Going out later with Dr. John for hookers and gumbo. Man, can he eat!

King Tut
Partyin' like a rock star in Hollywood, baby! Met up with the lads from Led Zep. Crazy stuff with a groupie and a fish. Debauchery of the road starting to get to me. Ah, who am I to judge? I was married to my sister.

King Tut
Heard the Steve Martin song on the radio last night. I get that he's a comedian and he has to make a living, but in my day there was respect for mummies. I get it; I'm hip. I wonder, though, how he'll feel when they write a little novelty song about his dead body. Oh, well. Haters gonna hate.

King Tut is at the **Seattle Art Museum**.

King Tut

All the towns starting to seem the same to me. You see inside one museum, you've seen inside them all. Just different paintings on the wall. Going to a drug-fueled orgy with the Mariners later. Hoping that'll cheer me up.

King Tut is at the **Metropolitan Museum of Art**.

King Tut

The city that never sleeps. Or maybe that's just me on all this cocaine, LOL. Thank you, Stevie Nicks! Beautiful lady, voice of an angel. Asked me to blow coke up her asshole. Hey, when you get a mummy and a witch together, all bets are off.

King Tut

America is just something I'm seeing through a bus window. And my sarcophagus eyeholes. Bob Seger had it right. Turn the page, man, turn the page.

King Tut is at **M. H. de Young Memorial Museum**.

King Tut

Selling a ton of merch here. Every kid in town has me on their T-shirt and a pocket full of drugs to slip me. I know I should be psyched but . . . fuck it. What does any of this shit really MEAN? Got some fresh air earlier on a trolley ride. Didn't help. Gonna detox when this is all over. Get a coupla colonics, go all Whole Earth–Euell Gibbons on y'all.

King Tut is at the **Art Gallery of Ontario**.

King Tut

Peace out, North America. I tried to give you what you wanted. Now I'm nothing but a hollowed-out shell of a man. I mean, I know that's what a mummy is, but still.

Monica Lewinski

Monica Lewinski
Anybody know how to get a stain out of a dress?

Linda Tripp You know who's really good with stains? Ken Starr. Probably you should give it to him.

Kenneth Starr likes this.

Bill Clinton I know how to get a stain on a dress LOL.

Monica Lewinski Bill! ROFL Gross!!

Bill Clinton You didn't think it was gross last night, didja?

Kenneth Starr LOL!

Kenneth Starr I mean, highly improper.

Hillary Clinton What are you guys talking about?

Bill Clinton Oh . . . Bosnia.

Lady Baby Gaga

 Lady Baby Gaga was Born This Way.

 Lady Baby Gaga likes **Madonna** and **Meat Diapers**.

 Lady Baby Gaga
Just learned to say my name today! Well, half of it.

 Lady Baby Gaga
Watching Muppet Babies. Thinking they would make nice clothes.

Lady Baby Gaga is friends with **Gay Babies**.

 Lady Baby Gaga
Just talked to Baby Beyoncé on the telephone.

 Baby Beyoncé likes this.

 Lady Baby Gaga Fisher-Price telephone, but still.

 Lady Baby Gaga likes Baby Shampoo.

 **Lady Baby Gaga** Tear free, and the bubbles are a great fashion idea.

Lady Baby Gaga posted a pic.

New mobile!!!

 Lady Baby Gaga Cute, but not enough offensive religious imagery.

Acknowledgments

Travis and Jonathan wish to thank Robyn von Swank, James Savage, the Harmons, the Shockleys, David Falk (who is great at Conquerville, BTW), Marcella Berger, Marie Florio, Martha Schwartz, Cherlynne Li, Ruth Lee-Mui, Michael Kwan, Emily Remes, Lance Koonce, Miya Kumangai, Sally Kim, Kevin McCahill, Amanda Demastus, Marcia Burch, Stacy Creamer, Jessica Roth (She's the title-iest!), Best Editor in History Lauren Spiegel for all the dirty talk, and Adrian Rose Leonard and Jenny Rainwater for letting us do this instead of being with them in any meaningful way.

About the Authors

TRAVIS HARMON and **JONATHAN SHOCKLEY** (aka Dr. Tony Cougar-mouth and Brylon K. Tilgh, Ph.D.) are the creators of the satirical web series Red State Update. Their videos have been viewed more than forty million times and the comedians have been featured in *USA TODAY*, *The Wall Street Journal*, and on CNN among other media outlets. They can be found at redstateupdate.com and youtube.com/travisandjonathan. Harmon and Shockley live in Los Angeles, California.

Photo Credits

Page	Description	Creator/Owner
1, 2	Two stars	Photo by NASA
5, 6	Serpent	Illustration by Travis Harmon
5	Women prohibited symbol	Antony McAulay/bigstock.com
5	Lion	Johan Swanepoel/bigstock.com
5	Apple	Edyta Pawlowska/bigstock.com
5	Lightning bolt	Miguel Angel Salinas Salinas/bigstock.com
15	Pyramids	Alexandr Belov/bigstock.com
15	Pharaoh	Amanda Lewis/bigstock.com
15	Slaves	Glen Gage/bigstock.com
15	Man with drill	Vuk Vukmirovic/bigstock.com
15	Alien	Georgios Kollidas/bigstock.com
18, 19, 20	Woman in costume	Kuznetsov Dmitry/bigstock.com
18	Cartoon pharaoh	Danilo Sanino/bigstock.com
18	Hat with stars	Slavoljub Pantelic/bigstock.com
20	Asp	Dakota / bigstock.com
24	Jet Ski	darren baker/bigstock.com
26	Volcano	Miguel Angel Salinas Salinas/bigstock.com
27, 28, 29	Man in striped shirt	Piotr Marcinski/bigstock.com
27, 28, 29	Hand with tall beer glass	Jason Stitt/bigstock.com
27, 28, 29	Hand with beer mug	Sergiy Tryapitsyn/bigstock.com
27, 28, 29	Hand with beer bottle	Jason Stitt/bigstock.com
27, 28, 29	Hand	Duncan Noakes/bigstock.com
33	Conquerville graphic	aloysius patrimonio/bigstock.com
34, 35, 36	Man in helmet	caesart /bigstock.com
37	Woman with microscope	Wavebreak Media Ltd/bigstock.com
39, 40, 41	Three heraldic lions	Speedfighter/bigstock.com
44	Mop and bucket	Brian J. Abela/bigstock.com
51	Buffalo	Steve Degenhardt/bigstock.com
51	Dinosaur	tmcnem/bigstock.com
51	Phone booth	Brent Hathaway/bigstock.com
52	Man with cigarette	john thielemann/bigstock.com
55	Turkey and stuffing	og-vision/bigstock.com
55	Seal	Keith Tarrier/bigstock.com
72	Raccoon	Eric Gevaert/bigstock.com

73, 74, 75, 76	Mustache (on raccoon)	Stephen Coburn/bigstock.com
73, 74, 75	Bowler (on raccoon)	Joachim Wendler/bigstock.com
75	Alamo	Christina DeRidder/bigstock.com
76	Sombrero (on raccoon)	Michale Flippo/bigstock.com
78, 79, 80, 81	California state silhouette	skvoor/bigstock.com
78, 79, 80, 81	Missouri state silhouette	skvoor/bigstock.com
87	Kangaroos	JinYoung Lee/bigstock.com
101	Man's chest	Photograph by CDC
110	Woman in cloche	RetroClipArt/bigstock.com
110	Cat in pajamas	studiodowney/shutterstock.com
110	Two men in bowlers	ArtPixz/bigstock.com
110	Liquor bottle	devon, AllSmileMedia/bigstock.com
110	Bathtub	Marko Beric/bigstock.com
110	Woman in black gloves	samodelkin8/shutterstock.com
111	Bull	Enrique Ramos López/bigstock.com
111	Subway sign	Speedfighter/bigstock.com
111	Lindy hoppers	Cenozoic Design/shutterstock.com
111	Mouse in boat	sahua d/shutterstock.com
112	Graph	Hermann Liesenfeld/bigstock.com
113, 114	Boy in bed	matka Wariatka/bigstockphoto.com
116, 117	Gavel	gibsonff/bigstock.com
117, 118	Monkey	Eric Isselée/bigstock.com
117	Jury	Konstantinos Kokkinis/bigstock.com
117	Man in judge's robes	Maria Carme Balcells/bigstock.com
118	Figure with question mark	Jose Gil/bigstock.com
119	Coffee cup	Pics Five/bigstock.com
119	Man with liquor bottle	Ljupco Smokovski/bigstock.com
119	Sihouette with liquor bottle	yurok aleksandrovich/bigstock.com
119	Bar sign	Mark Stout/bigstock.com
121, 122	U.S. country/flag	Donna Placente/bigstock.com
124, 125, 126	Rocket with dog	Kristina Afanasyeva/bigstock.com
124, 125, 126	Rocket launch	Pavel Losevsky/bigstock.com
128	Woman in white dress	Patrick Hermans/bigstock.com
128	Shirtless man with two women	Dmitry Parvanyan/bigstock.com
130	Woodstock poster	Lisa Fischer/bigstock.com
130	Puddle with raindrops	Morgan Rauscher/bigstock.com
130	Superimposed faces	Evan Sharboneau/bigstock.com
130	Man and woman	Scott Griessel/bigstock.com
130	Harmonica	Matthew Hadidian/bigstock.com
130	Hand with glass	Steve Cukrov/bigstock.com
130	Man with wineglass	Paula Wolf Borek/bigstock.com
130, 131, 132	Blue-lensed glasses	Ken Scribner/bigstock.com
130	Shoes	Nigel Silcock/bigstock.com
130	Deodorant bottle	Viktoriia Kulish/bigstock.com
131	Mouth and tongue	Ivanova Eleonora/bigstock.com
131	Guitar	Qi Zhou/bigstock.com
131	Sitars	Martijn Mulder/bigstock.com
131	Yoko Ono	Illustration by Adrian Rose
132	Man in yellow jacket	Janos Miseta/bigstock.com
132	Ringo Starr	Illustration by Adrian Rose
136, 137, 138	Dog	Deanna May/bigstock.com
139, 140	King Tut	Rachelle Burnside/bigstock.com
141	Tape recorder	RTimages the Photographer/bigstock.com
142	Baby	Vladimír Vítek/bigstock.com
142	Mobile	discpicture/shutterstock.com